SEVEN PRINCIPLES
for
RADIANT LIVING
by
Jason Chan

This first edition is published in the United Kingdom
in 2000 by The Radiant Health Foundation
21a Salisbury Road, Edinburgh, EH16 5AA

Edited by Victor Spence & Catriona Mitchell
Cover and Book Design: Kenneth Kerr
Photography: James Guilliam

Printed and bound in the United Kingdom by Bath Press

ISBN 0-9537818-0-1

ACKNOWLEDGEMENTS

With great appreciation and thanks I humbly bow to those beautiful co-life workers, who have dedicated their lives to bring Peace and Healing on our beloved Earth.

I give special thanks to Victor Spence, Dr Frank and Shirley Wilson, Kathie Harrison, Catriona Mitchell, Kenneth Kerr and James Guilliam for their editorial, design and photography and spiritual support.

Jason Chan

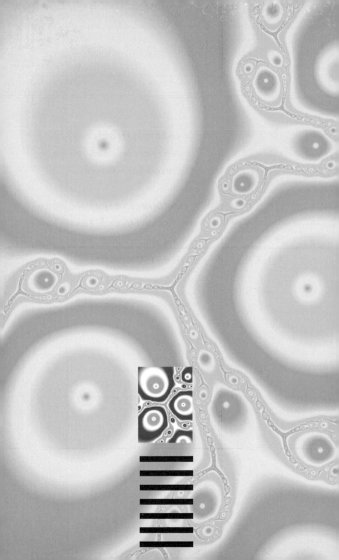

SEVEN PRINCIPLES for RADIANT LIVING

By JASON CHAN

INTRODUCTION

In the search for understanding and enlightenment in regard to the secrets of greater harmony in our lives and in the world, we are drawn toward those teachings that convey the sometimes deep but simple beauty of ancient wisdom. Presented here are seven principles based on this timeless wisdom. They will transform your life, forever.

Recommendations on how to use this book:

The gifts in this book are simple and practical. Start on a Sunday with the first principle, and finish the cycle with the seventh principle on a Saturday. Then simply repeat the process.

Alternatively, you can work specifically with one principle for a few days or even weeks so as to master that particular lesson. When you are happy with your progress, you can move on to harness the benefits of one of the other 'Principles for Radiant Living'.

1st PRINCIPLE

BELIEVE THAT YOU ARE THE MASTER
OF YOUR OWN LIFE

Can you believe that you are the master of your own life? Perhaps you'll need to put your rational mind to one side for a moment - your intellect and reason may be in conflict with this idea.

But you are already the master because you create your own reality.

There is no such thing as absolute truth, as long as perception lasts. We all hold different concepts of ourselves and the world around us, because we think, see and perceive things differently. So really, it is impossible to seek answers outside ourselves. It is up to each of us to look within, to find and know our personal truth. By doing this, you become your own master. You learn to create what it is that you really want in life.

We all want to be happy and fulfilled. But what really makes us happy? Many people yearn for fame and fortune; they live for the future in the hope that twenty years from now they'll finally get what they want. But life is day to day, moment to moment. Why pin your happiness on some point in the unforeseeable future?

You could try this instead: wake up in the mornings, and tell yourself, "No matter what happens in my life, I will be happy".

Decide it now.

Self-mastery requires taking responsibility for yourself, for what happens and has happened to you. You can no longer blame others for your life's circumstances, neither your parents, nor past lovers, not even society. You stand alone, and alone you face yourself and the world.

It may be especially hard to accept responsibility for your life when things are going badly, in your eyes - if you're sick or poor or in the middle of a divorce. But every situation comes with its opportunities.

If something is making you unhappy, you still have a choice: you can be victimized by it, depressed or angry, or you can choose to learn from the experience. As soon as you accept the part you've played in a challenging situation, you're less helpless. You then have the freedom to desire another outcome and make changes.

This is where your mastership comes in.

If you can change your perception, then, the mind is under control. It can serve you and its power is infinite.

Whether you realize it or not, the mind creates everything in your physical reality. The process begins with the mind directing energy in the form of thoughts. We transform food into energy, and energy into thought. Every thought we have influences every cell in our bodies, changing its chemistry. Just one change of thought changes our emotions and our physical make-up.

Thought turns into desire, and desire manifests through action. It is at this point that we can really help ourselves. We can harness our energy to create what we really want, by lightening and expanding our minds, and dreaming our wildest dreams. Then, depending on how strong our desire is, we can manifest our dreams into a physical reality. This is a miracle that is open to us all, only too often we don't see it.

We're too busy limiting ourselves with a narrow perception of who we are and what we're capable of.

We're too busy being the "old me".
There are two masters residing within each of us, and usually we try to serve both. The first is the ego-self, the concept of self which is limited. This self is an illusion; we invent it. It is the image we impose upon ourselves for a sense of identity. It is the mask we wear to face the world because without it we would not know who we are.

The ego-self is dependent on definitions and labels, on our names and status in life, our job titles and where we live. We spend a lot of time perfecting it, and because it is unnatural, we never feel truly at ease.

We are always reliant on superficial and above all transient things, which can burst like bubbles around us.

This kind of life is based on fear and insecurity.

Now let's look at the other self, the true self, or what is sometimes called the 'soul' or Higher Self. It is a point of consciousness which remains unchanged. Our personalities unfold day after day, year after year, and likewise our bodies develop and change, but still there is a "me" inside us that is the same at the age of three as it is at sixty-three. No job title, image, hairstyle or amount of money in the bank can define the true self. It exists without any visible identification, and its existence is beyond question. This self is our true master.

How do we recognize the true self?
It resides inside, always, in a state of grace, balance and beauty.

It is glorious and unique, and it likes to express its fine, creative qualities.

We find it when we experience inner peace, when our minds are open, when we are touched by the wonders of life, by immense beauty or joy, when we are moved by music, or gasp at a work of art which has resonance within. All of these moments are a union with the true self.

We definitely have two masters, and yet our minds cannot serve two masters at once. At every moment we can make the choice; either to serve the limited ego-self, built on all kinds of self-deception and illusion, or to serve the true self, a self based on love, compassion, wisdom and strength. It takes courage to express the true self, but the braver you are, the less you are subject to definition and limitation. The choice is yours.

If you really want to serve the true self, first you have to find it.

1st PRINCIPLE

BELIEVE THAT YOU ARE THE MASTER OF YOUR OWN LIFE.

The first principle is the most important. Let us examine what we are right now.

We are creating our own reality every moment of our lives, and it is necessary to know this truth, if we are to gain a deeper understanding of what it is to be human.

What we are now is a reflection of our past desires, will and deeds. In understanding this, now we must ask ourselves what we want from life, and what we can give. What we will do, or be, will then be determined by what our thoughts are.

Today's exercise and affirmation:

Sit quietly and observe your breath for a while. Breathe in rhythmically and gently. In your mind, say to yourself:

"I am the Master of my own life. I take and accept responsibility for my life, my thoughts, my desires and my deeds".

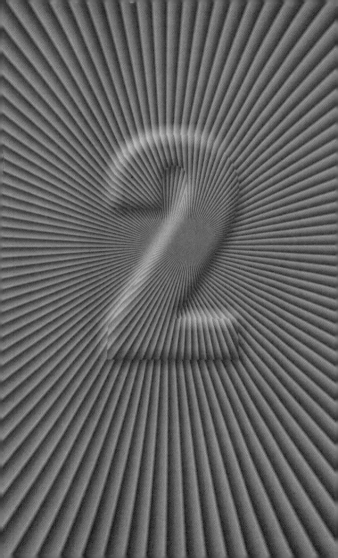

2nd PRINCIPLE

LET GO OF THE PAST
AND EMBRACE THE PRESENT

If you wish to realize your fullest potential, and live a life that is joyous and free, **you have to learn to live in the moment.** This can be a challenging task, as it means relinquishing the past, and welcoming the unknown. This is the only way to unleash the true self. The master within can only exist in the here-and-now, and remains obscured when the mind associates too much with its past conditioning.

Conditioning is based on many things, on where you were born, what sort of house you lived in, your upbringing, education, parental influences and beliefs, and so on. All of these things have taught you how to act in the world. They have made you into who you are, what you believe, even how you physically look. And yet you need not let them limit you or prevent you from being who you want to be today.

Most people live in the past, for reasons of "security". Some dwell in the future, but really the future is an illusion, a mere projection of past experiences. Somehow we believe that if we cling to what we already know, we will be safe and free from suffering. But all our fears, worries and anxieties come from the past. By holding onto them we are keeping them alive.

This is not to say that you should get rid of all your memories. Let go of the things that imprison you.

You must identify the barriers you've built up, if you want to learn to be open.

Your core beliefs and patterns will be so deeply embedded that they are beyond your conscious awareness.

It is time to make them conscious. It's time to embark on a fantastic journey of self-discovery.

Let's take an example of the power of conditioning. Imagine your parents told you consistently while you were growing up, that you were an ugly duckling. By the time you were twelve years old, this would have become a very strong affirmation in your life. Objectively, when you look in a mirror now, you might see that you are not ugly. But after many years of conditioning, it would be natural to believe that you are.

If someone tells you now that you are beautiful, you will not believe them. You might even react in an ugly way, unable to take the compliment, thus reinforcing your belief in your own ugliness!

When you live a theory, it becomes your truth. So be careful!

Know what your theories are!

You can identify your conditioning by using the present as a tool. It is a mirror, which tells you about yourself. Examine your daily self. Get to know and understand your subconscious patterns. How do you react to yourself? How do you respond to the world? Behave like a detective, looking for clues as to who you are. Which patterns are destructive? Which prevent you from being the person you really want to be?

Let go of everything that is unloving or unforgiving. Whatever hinders your progress has to go.

Our minds and subconscious are usually so full of outdated concepts and conditioning, that nothing new can enter. There is simply no room! This creates a life that is blocked. Until you have cleared some space and opened yourself to receiving, you will experience no new moments. You will interpret everything according to your past, and reinforce old limitations, creating more of the same. You are unable to move forward.

Let go of the old to make way for the new. Let go of the past, and embrace the present! Forgiveness is vital in the letting go process. Every single person in your past has to be let go of and forgiven. Eventually, if you can forgive the world, you are free. You are no longer imprisoned.

Gradually, as you learn the art of letting go, you will be amazed at how your relationships blossom. Jealousy, guilt and insecurity will dissipate as you let go of your fear of past hurts and imagination.

You will become whole, and cease to need too much from others.

Instead of imprisoning your loved ones with your fears, you will allow them to be whole too, and you will learn to fly together.

Without your past, you don't have to behave as you were told or expected to. You can be your own person.

Suddenly you'll become as natural as the air you breathe, as free as the wind, as light as the sky! Imagine what this could feel like!

When you make room for your inner master, by clearing your past to embrace the present, you'll suddenly find you have a purpose - a higher purpose which transcends all the limitations you have imposed on yourself. Every morning when you wake up, you'll know somewhere deep inside that there's a dream for you to fulfil, and no-one else can do it for you. Only you can, and it is the reason you are here. Do not waste a single moment!

2nd PRINCIPLE

LET GO OF THE PAST AND EMBRACE THE PRESENT.

We are continually influenced by our subconscious conditions. Through the journey of life, we are not influenced by positive and good patterns alone. It is therefore important to embark on a journey of clearing our collected unfavourable patterns and conditioning if we want to live fully here and now.

Today's exercise and affirmation:

Sit in peace, observe your breath for a while, and find a quiet place in your mind. Breathe in rhythmically and gently.
In your mind, say to yourself:

"I let go of the past.
It no longer serves my higher purpose".
(Repeat this at least three times).

In carrying out this exercise, you can be specific to any problem, relationship difficulty, unworthy image, etc. It may take days, weeks or months just to release one old fixed pattern.

3rd PRINCIPLE

I WILL BE
KIND TO MYSELF

Be kind to yourself at all times. This may sound obvious, but really, it is not as easy as it sounds. We are often our own worst enemy. Being kind and compassionate, especially to oneself, is a skill that needs to be nurtured and developed. It requires both application and dedication.

This is because, in order to be kind to yourself, you have to accept yourself as you are, and not as you would like to be. People very rarely accept themselves without judgments or conditions, and this is where we can create our own problems and unhappiness. Remember that through your perception, you are the creator of your own universe. You decide what is acceptable and what is not.

So be gentle, and forgive yourself for your shortcomings.

Examine how you treat yourself. Are you too harsh? Perhaps you have high expectations of yourself, and want to leave your mark on the world. If so, congratulations! But be sure your motives are driven by love. The urge to over-work can be a disguised desire for self-punishment or self-victimization. It is always aiming at some perceived reward in the future, and prevents you from living, and loving, now.

If you want to learn to be kind to yourself, then you must transcend your own guilt. Guilt often gets in the way of self-acceptance, and as soon as we have invited it into our lives, we have stopped loving ourselves. We feel worthless and belittled. Quite often we inherit guilt from childhood. How can we be kind to ourselves when we are full of unpleasant feelings from such an early age?

Some religions say we are born with sin, and if you believe this, you really have no choice but to feel worthless!
It is uncomfortable for us to harbour guilt.

Usually we deal with it by finding a scapegoat. We project our feelings onto other people, thus unburdening ourselves, and we experience a temporary release. This is a vicious, and destructive, circle. Guilt asks for punishment, and through projection, punishment is achieved.

We are all playing emotional and mental games. We are experts at it. For instance, when we fall in love, we manipulate our partners. If we feel jealous or angry, suffer from self-pity or co-dependency, we accuse the other and blame them for making us feel this way. We tell them it is their fault; that if they behaved differently we would not feel like this.

Really we are trying to make them guilty for our own feelings of worthlessness.

This allows us to avoid taking responsibility for our own well-being. But if you are kind to yourself, there is no need to go through all this!

Guilt plays a large role in family dynamics. If parents feel inadequate at raising their children, they berate themselves, and their family lives become tense - and all in the name of love! Guilt also underlies the behaviour of parents who overcompensate and spoil their children with sweets or toys.

Children are very astute; when they know their parents feel guilty, they learn to manipulate for what they want.

This benefits no-one, really, because where there is guilt, there is no expression of love.

The way we see and treat ourselves is the way we see and treat others.

Look back into your life and you will find this to be true. If you are very strict and well-disciplined, you will expect others to be likewise. If you are cruel to yourself and tend towards self-punishment, then you might be cruel in turn to others.

But then, if you are kind to yourself, you will be accepting and compassionate towards the rest of the world.

There are many ways you can practise self-love. Start with your physical body. Take care not only with your physical appearance, but with your internal organs! Pay attention to your diet.

Eat whole foods. The food you eat affects your emotions, so make sure you are nurturing yourself properly.

Take time for yourself each day. Time in which to relax, and more importantly, to breathe! Being conscious of your breath is the single most nurturing thing you can do. Use your nose or your mouth, it is up to you. But breathe, consciously, for fifteen minutes per day initially, and then a little longer.

This breathing practice will give you strength. It will enable you to look at your fears without needing to run away and hide, or fall into old patterns. It will release blockages, and help you to let go and forgive, so that you can become sensitized to your true self. It will reunite you with the life force, with God, if you like. It is a very healing pursuit.

As well as your daily breathing practice, give yourself a reward, at least once a week. Enjoy a bubble-bath by candlelight, or buy a bottle of champagne, and enjoy each sip. Do something that symbolises a celebration of life. Spoil yourself a little!

As you nurture yourself, remarkable changes will occur in your life. Peace, love and compassion will grow within you, and you will begin to share this special energy. People will start to respond to you, perhaps see you in a completely new way, and they will want to get close to you.

Your life will become fuller, and richer. You may feel you cannot afford the time to give completely to yourself. But really, nothing could be of greater importance. If you really want to be successful in life, nurture yourself, physically, emotionally and mentally. Love yourself always. Then you can truly learn to share your love, with yourself and with others.

3rd PRINCIPLE

I WILL BE KIND TO MYSELF.

Many people do not know how to love themselves, let alone share love with others. It is very important to take time off to nurture ourselves, physically, emotionally and mentally.

There are ways you can practise being kind to yourself. Tai-Chi gentle movement for grace and beauty, Chi-Kung Chinese breathing art for inner strength, Yoga for physical strength and flexibility, relaxation and meditation to heal our hearts and minds and to nurture the soul – all of these are beneficial.

If we really want to be successful in life we must care for ourselves, and love ourselves always.

Today's exercise and affirmation:

Sit quietly with your back straight and observe your breath for a while. Use your nose to breathe in and your mouth to breathe out. When you are ready, in your mind say to yourself:

"I nurture myself. I look after my physical body, nurture my feelings and take time to clear my mind".

To assist us further, to nurture our feelings and calm the mind, we can use this additional meditative affirmation and simple breathing exercise:

Sit quietly and observe your breath for a short while. Breathe in slowly and hold for three seconds. Continue this breathing cycle and as you breathe in, imagine you are sitting on a mountain-top watching the sunrise. Breathe in the mountain breeze to clear and still your mind.

At the same time, let the fresh breeze wash your emotions.

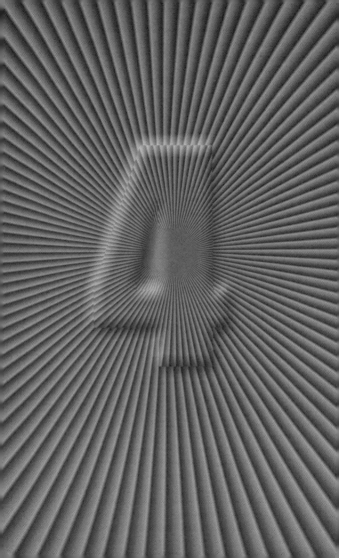

4th PRINCIPLE

To Give
Is To Receive

As you give, you receive. This is universal law; a great law of cause and effect that Eastern teaching calls Karma. It is as natural as the movement of air and water. Every time you give, you receive, whether it be a kindness, a sum of money, or your time.

Everything is energy, including yourself. If energy is not moving it stagnates - just like a stagnant pond, where the water is still and the energy has gone stale.

Energy needs to flow to stay fresh and alive. This is why the stream flows continuously to the river, and the river to the sea. When there is no exchange of energy, there is death.

This is why, for our well-being, it is essential that we learn to give and receive properly, so that our energy can flow without becoming blocked.

Money is energy. Dealing with money is great practice for giving and receiving. Observe what happens to you when you are handling money. How do you react? How do you use money? How do you feel when you pay your bills?

If you struggle with money, if it seems you never have enough, or if money occupies your mind more than anything else, try to adopt a different attitude towards it. Do not make it your enemy! Accomplish the natural law, instead. Create money, and give it out, keeping things moving. Create a vortex of energy. When you do spend money, for example when you pay your bills, do not do it grudgingly. Appreciate the service you are paying for, and bless the whole procedure. Do it with an inner smile.

You will be making people happy, and at the same time helping the wheel go round.

I keep two special baskets in my meditation room. In one, I place my unpaid bills, and in the other, all the money and cheques I receive. When the outgoings are greater than what's coming in, I look into my life to see where I am blocked, and in my meditation I ask for these fears and worries to be removed.

Very rarely are these concerns to do with the unpaid bills; they are due more to my attitude towards them. Through this I have no financial worries. Try it out!

I also bless all the money I receive, sending appreciation to the people involved, thanking them for all they have given me. I ask the universe to return their giving, and to increase it a hundred-fold.

Trust that you will always have enough money. Never say "I can't afford it". As soon as you say that, it is true. Try saying instead, "I am very rich but I do not have enough cash coming in as yet to pay for it". When you can do this, you will never be poor. This will take months, even years, of practice, but it is well worth it!

The laws of giving and receiving do not only apply to money. Try giving and receiving with love and kindness. Support other people; let their success become yours. Do not entertain envy or jealousy. Helping others to create abundance will help you to create your own abundance.

If you want to be cared for, try caring for someone else. If you want to be loved, try loving someone else. Do not forget: whatever you give out will come back.

You will learn a lot about yourself and your attitudes while practising this. You will heal yourself by encouraging your energy to flow, and getting rid of your blockages. But be prepared for interference from your ego! It will try to get in the way. It will tell you, for instance, that you are too poor to buy someone a present.

Yet presents do not have to cost money. You can give a feather, a stone from the beach, a plant from your garden: give it in love and it will cost you nothing. **You do not have to be rich to give. You just need a big heart.**

From the ego-self's point of view, giving means losing. This may be why, so often, we withhold our life force. We become selective in our giving, and impose conditions on it. This way it ceases to be giving at all; it becomes bargaining, or bartering, as we expect something back in exchange. There is a big and important difference between bargaining and giving, which we have to learn.

This is particularly true in intimate relationships. Often we have been brought up to dream of that special person to whom we can give our love. But we bring a host of expectations to that person. A romance like this is based on fantasy. It involves bargaining, and does not last. It soon becomes clear that our chosen one does not fill the emptiness within us. Time and time again we try to fill this empty hole with romantic love, and again and again we are disappointed.

We must learn to give and to flow naturally like the movements of Tai Chi. When doing Tai Chi you feel good because you move in harmony. There is no bargaining. As you open yourself to the flow of energy, life force increases and you find it easy to give kindness and love without reservation. You find you really care for others' welfare based on natural kindness and without ulterior motives.

You cannot give what you do not have. This is why you must be kind to yourself. Love yourself, and you will be eager to give your love without any bargaining, even to complete strangers. And the more you give, the more you will receive. Experiment; you will find that this law does not fail. Life will become richer than you could ever imagine.

4th PRINCIPLE

TO GIVE IS TO RECEIVE.

As we give, we receive: this is universal law,
a great law that Eastern teaching calls
Karma (cause and effect).

If you want happiness,
learn to give happiness.
If you want respect, learn to
respect others.
If you want to be rich,
help others to be rich.
If you want peace, then teach peace.
If you want love, learn to love
others unconditionally.

Today's exercise and affirmation:

Sit quietly with your back straight and observe your breath for a while. Use your nose to breathe in and your mouth to breathe out. When you are ready in your mind, say to yourself:

"Everywhere I go, I give the gift of a smile to the people I meet".

Remember to greet people with joy and respect. Help others to succeed. Demonstrate confidence and peace in everyday life.

Also remember to receive joy, fun, happiness, love and respect from the people in your life.

5th PRINCIPLE

I WILL
BE STILL ON A DAILY BASIS, INVESTING
IN HAPPINESS AND INNER JOY

We all have a wise and true master within. But in the modern world, we are inundated with information from outside, and the pace of our lives can be frantic. From the moment we wake up in the mornings, our minds are in motion, planning the day, worrying about yesterday, and tomorrow.

We are confused, out of balance and out of control. Under these circumstances it is impossible to stay in touch with the true self.

This is why it is so important to be still, on a daily basis. Being still puts you in touch with your source. It enables you to clear away the debris in your mind, to create some space. You already have the answers to all of your questions.

You need to create the stillness, the emptiness, which allows your deep inner voice, guidance and insight, to be revealed.

Meditation is the most effective way of practising stillness. It calms the mind, relaxes the physical body, and stills the emotions. It is a dive into the depths of the mind, as opposed to a struggle on its surface. It provides a state of deep relaxation and clarity.

As all great artists and inventors testify, it is these moments of clarity which lead to life's most inspired moments.

There are many different meditation methods, and whether you use a mantra, a point of focus, or concentrate on your breathing, the important thing is to do it regularly. Set aside a quiet place for your practice. Always meditate when you are fresh and not tired, and sit in a good posture with your back straight. The ideal position is the lotus, but if you prefer, then sit on a straight-backed chair.

Meditation works primarily by passing through the inner chatter which distracts us, to reveal inner peace and silence. Thoughts come and go, but if we attach no importance to them, then the turbulence subsides, and gradually the mind settles down into its natural, calm state.

It becomes like a still pond, able to reflect the graceful state of your true self.

Meditating heightens your perception and awareness, so you can tell the difference between your true self and your ego-self. It gives you perspective on your problems, as everything falls into place. All sickness, hatreds and jealousies fade away, and it becomes easier to forgive.

In many ways meditation is a process of "unlearning", and an opportunity to re-educate yourself. It clears your mind of past "junk", of things that have contaminated you - gossip, violence, resentments and fear. Provided that you do not gather more in the present, you are free.

At times, meditation may become challenging, and you will want to reject yourself, give in to fear, compose shopping lists, even fall asleep to avoid facing yourself! But you cannot escape from who you truly are.

Remember it is only your ego-self, behaving like an uncooperative and rebellious child, which is making the process trying. Persist, and you'll receive insights and benefits which you will never loose. They are your greatest inheritance.

Each time you practise, you will reach your inner stillness. To begin with it may only be for a moment, but you will learn to attain it for longer and longer. The more you meditate, the more the inner peace infuses your being and becomes part of you. Eventually it will become your way of life and whether you are skiing or cooking, you will be in contact with your true source all the time. You will find yourself strengthened - external chaos may still surround you, but you will become less and less affected by it. You will remain tranquil and serene in the face of any storm, with the knowledge that your safety lies within you.

Remember that meditation is a state of 'non-doing', which is subtly different from a state of doing nothing. It is not about suppression, or passivity. When your mind is busy, you spend your life copying others, you are not natural, and you aren't really doing anything. Your life force is scattered in all directions.

When you are empty, on the other hand, your mind is open and it is at these times that you are most receptive.

You can feel your energy, your chi, and truly direct it to get the results you want. Seek emptiness, and you will discover the infinite creative potential in your life.

Perhaps meditation does not appeal to you. If this is the case, then try to find other means of inviting stillness into your life. If you are religious, say a prayer. Or simply indulge in contemplation of nature - look at the sun, the moon, or passing clouds. Walk in the country, listen to music, or play golf , but whatever you do, empty your mind. Free it from all petty, daily concerns.

You cannot live to your full potential until you learn the art of being still inside. Practise it, every day, and let it become your strength. Stillness will cultivate the depth inside you and enable you to express your best qualities to the world. You will discover your true being, your creativity, and your enormous capacity for peace, contentment, and love.

5th PRINCIPLE

"I WILL BE STILL ON A DAILY BASIS, INVESTING IN HAPPINESS AND INNER JOY".

It is not the function of our minds to think and work all of the time.
All great artists and musicians know that one secret to their creativity is to have a clear mind, before a great moment of inspiration can occur.

Today's exercise and affirmation:

"I am still and at peace".

To meditate, be at one with your breath. Relax, and breathe rhythmically and gently.

Use some gentle music and tune into nature. Bring an inner smile to your heart. Learn to be still, not busy. You can also use this stillness for a moment of self-reflection. Allow life to show you the way.

A precious moment of genuine stillness can show us the beauty of life.

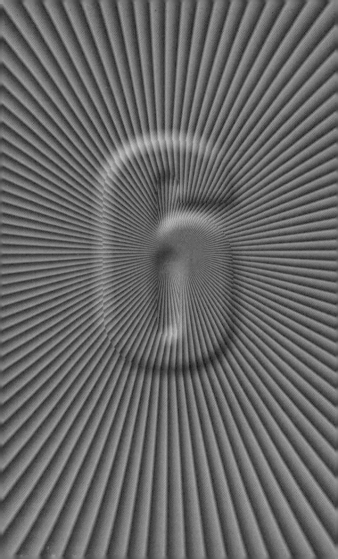

6th PRINCIPLE

APPRECIATION WILL INCREASE,
AND CONDEMNATION WILL MULTIPLY

Your happiness and well-being depend entirely on your perception of the world. Are you an optimist, or a pessimist? Do you see your cup as half empty, or half full?

It is useful to observe how much you appreciate, and how much you condemn, the world around you; because, ultimately, it is you who decides what the world is like.

Learn the art of appreciation. Work at it a little, and it will improve your life enormously. Appreciate your day, appreciate your time. If you allow eight hours for sleep, then you still have sixteen hours every day to play around with. How are you going to spend them? It is all free will and free choice: what can you do to fill your day in the most beautiful and fulfilling of ways?

The first thing to appreciate when you wake up in the morning, is your aliveness! How many people open their eyes and groan: "Oh no, another day, how awful", and try desperately to go back to sleep? Appreciate the fact that you are still alive, as, really, when you go to sleep, you never know if you will wake up again or not. Every new day is a miracle!

At present you are experiencing the world with your physical body. When you pass away, you will be in a different dimension, and maybe you will miss all the physical sensations of this existence. So appreciate your senses, the taste of your toothpaste, the morning sunlight, the scenery you see on your way to work.

Try not to take these things for granted, just because they are familiar.

Appreciate your family, and your friends. This is extremely important, because you become more alive when you appreciate the people around you, and they will keep coming close to you. When you learn the art of appreciation, you learn the art of true friendship. You will offer support without judgment, without condemnation.

And then people will sense this; they will feel the abundance and compassion you wish to share, because it is overflowing in you, and they will open like flowers around you. Your life will be full of heart-to-heart exchanges.

Bear in mind one thing - we are all very lonely. Most people are too concerned with their own pettiness or triviality, to give their time to each other, and social interaction is reduced to dinner parties or a round of golf. Genuine appreciation will show you a different, more intimate way, and people will like you, forever, because you are not judging them. They will appreciate you in return for your appreciation.

Appreciation will increase as you practise it, becoming a more and more potent force in your life. But the converse is also true: condemnation will multiply. As appreciation brings love and well-being, condemnation brings ills and illusion, and makes you weak, angry and stiff.

Condemnation is based on judgments, and when you make this choice it becomes your reality. The more you condemn a person or the world, the worse they will become. When you judge someone, they will run away from you, because nobody likes to be condemned or judged. So try your best, do not try to change others, try to find the goodness in them. It is hard, but it will fill your cup up with goodness, until it overflows, and then you have a lot to give. It is then that you can really live life fully.

If you prolong condemnation, you actually deny your own happiness. Yes, the weather is awful sometimes. But if you are your own master, you can find the sunshine from within all the time. This is why you must learn to be still, to find the warmth inside. Use candlelight, use music, talk to people who are like-minded, hold people's hands, and appreciate your moment-to-moment living.

Try a little experiment. Spend one whole day consciously appreciating everything that you receive.

Appreciate being alive, and everything that you experience during the day. Then, force yourself to do the opposite: condemn everything for a day. This task may well be the easier of the two: there is plenty to complain about, if you look for it - crime, pollution, cold weather, bad programmes on the television, nothing in the fridge, and so on.

In both cases, observe what happens. What can you ascertain from your experiences? Which method feels better? This experiment will produce the same results time and time again.

Whatever you find within, you find without. That is the law of perception. When you find love within, you see a lovely world. When you find hatred within, you see everybody as enemies. So, cultivate appreciation. It may take effort, but the effort will be utterly worthwhile, as it will become a joy.

Above all, remember: do not try to change the world; first, try to change yourself. Follow these principles, and you will lead a life blessed with love, riches, and radiant health.

6th PRINCIPLE

"APPRECIATION WILL INCREASE;
CONDEMNATION WILL MULTIPLY".

If you give more thanks in your life, you will see a more thankful world. Say 'thank you' from your heart. Say 'thank you' when you wake up in the morning, say 'thank you' before you go to sleep, and give more thanks in between.

Today's exercise and affirmation:

"I appreciate my life and give thanks..."

Try for one whole day to be appreciative of a simple cup of tea, appreciate a given smile, appreciate your meal, appreciate that thoughtful gesture, and appreciate a kind word. Be aware of eliminating as much condemnation as possible.

Observe how you feel and watch the reactions of the people around you. The world will rejoice with you.

Appreciation will increase.

To further this exercise, you should try for one day to condemn everything in sight and mind. You will become very aware that the world will no longer be rejoicing with you. Condemnation will multiply.

Compare the difference between appreciating everything and condemning everything. Ask yourself which exercise feels best.
The answer will be swift and clear.

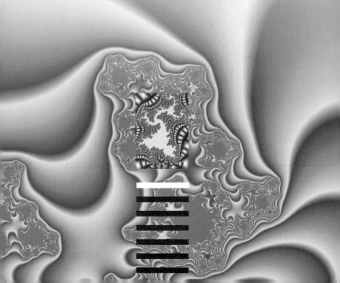

7th PRINCIPLE

I LIVE IN
A WORLD OF ABUNDANCE

Most people live as though the world is built on lack. They go from day to day finding that they do not have enough love, money, power or vitality - and they struggle through life trying to grab as much as they can, convinced that survival and success are a struggle.

And yet if you look into these people's lives, you see that they appear to have plenty. Their homes may be full of clothes, shoes and objects that they do not even use, and they have family and friends. There is an assumption underlying their complaints: it says that our planet is so small, the resources so scarce, that there simply is not enough to go round.

Their problems lie not in lack, but in the perception of lack.

Are you susceptible to feelings of lack? Perhaps, like many, you have had a poverty consciousness all your life. If so, it will have become a very strong affirmation by now. Without even realizing it, you will be giving it more power all the time. How many times a day do you tell yourself, "Oh, no, I can't afford that. It's too expensive"? Belief in scarcity will become a self-fulfilling prophecy.

If feelings of lack are familiar to you, it is time to change your perception.

Turn your principle of lack into the principle of abundance.

Never let fear of scarcity take hold.

Abundance is not actually about how much you have. It is a state of being. It is directly related to your confidence, to how good you feel about the here-and-now. That is why it is so important to let go of your past. Lack and poverty are caused by your conditioning, and anything that has undermined your sense of self-esteem has to be let go. Know that your worth is unlimited. Remove all images of unworthiness in yourself.

You are whatever you believe, feel and desire at any given moment.

Understanding this is the key to an abundant life. We all have inner richness, and the true self always wants to create abundance. It is vital, then, that we are in constant communication with that part of ourselves. Being still on a daily basis will help you to transform your consciousness.

Identifying the areas of lack in your life is the first step towards change. When you know what you want, then you can go about creating it. But saying "I want to be rich" is not good enough. You can only become rich by being it. Imagine how it feels to be rich.

It is likely that at some point in your past, you experienced a moment of richness - not necessarily in financial terms; perhaps you received a gift, fell in love, or were forgiven by somebody. Recall the feeling. Did you feel lighter? Did you have more positive fantasies about what you could do with your future, your career, and so on? Were you more creative, more generous, and less calculating? Cultivate these feelings of richness as much and as often as you can.

Inner cultivation will lead to outer manifestation. The deeper you go into yourself, the more abundance will be yours. The universe is a place of plenty, and it actually wants to provide us with abundance. We just have to create the momentum.

Practise an active affirmation of abundance, every day, in your meditation, and by sharing what you have. Try using ten percent of your income to give unconditionally. Even if are temporarily unemployed, give loose change to people in need. You will not feel poorer for it. It will help you relinquish your habit of poverty, and when you can cultivate this state of being, you know you are very rich, even if you have no cash on you.

Letting go of your belief in lack will have immediate and very positive repercussions. Suddenly you will find you can give freely. Suddenly, you will have time to be still, to let go and nurture yourself. You will find that health, wealth, friendship and love enter your life as if by magic. You will give off an air of abundance, and people will want to know your secret.

Tell them, simply, "I changed my mind".

The world is crying out for a belief in abundance. Imagine how crime could be reduced! People steal to make themselves richer. They believe the world does not have enough for them, and yet they do not realize that every time they steal, they affirm their own belief that they are very poor.

If all the world's thieves understood they live in a world of abundance, they would not need to steal at all.

First, perception needs to change, then feeling and action will follow.

Do you doubt that the world really is abundant? If so, remember that your mind is the ultimate creative agent. Whatever you perceive, you receive. When your mind is rich in abundance, it has to manifest. There is no other way. Do not under-estimate the power of "abundant thinking". It will change your life, forever.

7th PRINCIPLE

I LIVE IN A WORLD OF ABUNDANCE.

Every time we feel that we should withhold our giving, we are affirming that "this is a world of scarcity".

This is the principle of 'lack', and by affirming this principle in our lives, we acclaim that "I do not have enough, so I cannot share and cannot give".

What we believe (affirm), is the reality that we project into the world.

Today's exercise and affirmation:

Sit quietly with your back straight and observe your breath for a while. Use your nose to breathe in and your mouth to breathe out. When you are still and at peace, in your mind, say to yourself:

"I live in a world of abundance".

Find the sunshine that lies within you, that glowing and powerful light that will banish all darkness. By re-affirming abundance in your life, you are changing your mind.

See great loving relationships in your life.

Be radiant with health, full of fun and friendship. See money as energy and see this energy flowing through you.

Visualise people being loving, friendly, and full of joy toward you.

Visualise yourself being loving, friendly and full of joy toward others.

...and finally:

You are now holding the keys to successful, happy, joyful, peaceful and abundant living. All that you need to do now is practise these seven principles, and be your highest potential.

With best wishes, love and blessings,

Jason Chan